T0209832

THE REALITY OF
GOD'S
LOVE

Carol Sparks

WESTBOW
PRESS®
A DIVISION OF THOMAS NELSON
& ZONDERVAN

WestBow Press books may be ordered through booksellers or by contacting:

WestBow Press
A Division of Thomas Nelson & Zondervan
1663 Liberty Drive
Bloomington, IN 47403
www.westbowpress.com
1 (866) 928-1240

ISBN: 978-1-9736-2674-9 (sc)
ISBN: 978-1-9736-2673-2 (e)

Library of Congress Control Number: 2018904844

Print information available on the last page.

WestBow Press rev. date: 5/3/2018

Foreword

Over the decades, much has been preached, taught, and written about God's love, but very little scriptural truth has been revealed about it.

The Bible is where God's character and the basic concepts of godly love are revealed to humankind. For the most part, Christians are comfortable with the beliefs that have developed about this feature of God's character.

Christians often claim that because God is love, he loves everyone; he loves us because he created us, he loves us from birth, he loves us equally and unconditionally, and he will never stop loving us.

We in the Christian community do not question any aspect of these principles and reject any argument to the contrary. We reason that our beliefs are true because that is what we have been told, and we rarely question what we are told.

Because we don't want to offend anyone by mentioning the subject of sin, we have turned this single godly attribute into our gospel message. However, the simple message "God loves you" does nothing to convey the need for a personal Savior.

The concept of God's love is woefully misrepresented throughout the corporate church. Consequently, we have effectively altered God's character and diminished his holiness and sovereignty. As a result, we have become complacent about others' salvation. We function on our comfort level and have settled for lifestyles in which our relationship with God has lost its significance.

Much of our spiritual knowledge is derived from a steady diet of soft sermons and introspective reading material rather than on God-centered teaching designed to illuminate spiritual truths and stimulate growth.

We have become a community of believers with little depth of understanding focused on our needs and what God can do for us; we are convinced we are in good standing with the Lord.

In this book, we will explore our beliefs about godly love by examining the spiritual truth in scripture. Scripture in this book is paraphrased or quoted from the NIV Life Application Study Bible. I hope you will find this enlightening and thought provoking as the Holy Spirit leads you through this fascinating study.

Contents

Foreword v

Chapter 1   God Is Love.. 1
Chapter 2   God Loves Us because He Created Us............. 4
Chapter 3   God Loves Everyone...................................... 9
Chapter 4   God Loves Us Equally.................................. 14
Chapter 5   God Loves Us Unconditionally..................... 18
Chapter 6   God Will Never Stop Loving Us.................... 23
Chapter 7   In His Name 27
Chapter 8   When He Returns 31
Chapter 9   We Will Be Judged....................................... 35

CHAPTER 1

God Is Love

God is love. Whoever lives in love lives in God, and God in them.
—1 John 4:16

Let's start by delving into the meaning of this scripture starting with the first three words, *God is love.*

God refers to the eternal creator (Psalm 90:2; Isaiah 40:28), and the word *is* is to make something evident, to point out, or give knowledge of something invisible, a form of the word (be: to exist, have reality). *Is* gives evidence to the existence of God's love and expresses the knowledge of the invisible characteristic in the omniscient, omnipresent, and omnipotent God.

Am is another form of the word *be*—greatness, abundance, largeness, unstressed, not subjected to physical, psychological, or emotional pressure; "I AM WHO I AM" (Exodus 3:14 NIV). The eternal, invisible, present, self-existent Creator and sustainer of life is never stressed or pressured.

YHWH/YAHWEH—God's personal name is a verb meaning "to be," a continuous action.

God is a continual reality in our lives working in us and through us. *Love* is something that cannot be seen. Its components include:

- emotion—feeling, sentiment, sensation, passion
- virtue—desirable quality, kindness, affection
- attitude or mind-set—a way of thinking or behaving

- characteristic—a feature that distinguishes or represents a person
- force—an invisible power in our lives

Love is a tender affection, kindness, and personal attachment to someone. It seeks the best interests of others regardless of their actions.

Some other godly characteristics include the following.

- **compassion**—pity, sympathy, or understanding for the suffering of others often including a desire to help: "The Lord is full of compassion and mercy" (James 5:11 NIV); Because of His goodness, the Lord shows compassion to everyone (Psalm 145:8–9).
- **mercy**—kindness or forgiveness shown to someone. Because of His kindness and love, we are saved by His mercy (Titus 3:4).
- **forgiveness**—to pardon and release from the penalty for wrongdoing. Everyone who believes in the name of Jesus receives forgiveness (Acts 10:43). God is faithful and just and will forgive our confessed sins (1 John 1:9).
- **grace**—the unearned favor of God that provides for our salvation. We are justified by His grace (Romans 3:24); the Lord is compassionate, gracious, slow to anger, and abounding in love (Psalm 103:8).

Love is probably the most identifiable of God's virtues. It brings joy, contentment, comfort, and peace. It is the unseen force that gives meaning to our lives.

Summary

Love is one component of God's character. God cannot be pressured into doing anything outside His character or will. He is, however, not a slave to what He created. "I will have mercy on whom I will have mercy, and I will have compassion on whom I will have compassion" (Exodus 33:19 NIV).

This verse suggests that not everyone is a recipient of God's mercy and compassion.

Conclusion

God's invisible quality of love is an attribute, not an obligation.

Question

What is the deciding factor for those who will or will not receive mercy and compassion from God?

CHAPTER 2

God Loves Us because He Created Us

God is Spirit
—John 4:24

Humanity was made in the likeness of God (Genesis 1:26–31). God is divine spirit while humanity is human spirit. The spirit is the fundamental requirement for life. It cannot be seen, but we can see the evidence of the spirit through our and others' character and disposition. Every human spirit was created before the beginning of time.

Before the creation of the world, God created humanity's spirit. He knew who would receive his Son (Ephesians 1:4).

It's important to recognize the sequence of creation. God created humanity's spirit when nothing else existed. We were created to be in a personal relationship with the Father. Every other relationship is secondary to the one we have with God. He knew us before we were conceived; he knew us before we were born (Jeremiah 1:5).

God knows us by our spirit, which gives us personal identities. The world was created as a place for us to express our individual character. Before we were born, God knew the way we would live and the choices we would make.

After the creation of humanity's spirit, God created the heavens and the earth (Genesis 1:1–25).

Day 1

He separated the light from the darkness and called them day and night—the natural rhythm of time began with the first evening and morning. This time frame refers to hours, not centuries or millennia.

Day 2

He separated the water from the sky.

Day 3

He separated the water from the land and created every kind of plant and tree.

Day 4

He created the sun, moon, and stars.

Day 5

He created all the creatures of the sea and the birds of the air.

Day 6

He created all the land animals, including insects. God created man and woman and gave them everything they needed for their existence. He placed man in the Garden of Eden and put him in charge of everything He had created (Psalm 8:6–8).

Genesis 2:7 describes how God formed man from the earth and breathed life into him. The Hebrew word for breath is *ruwach*; it is synonymous with *blow*, *wind*, and *spirit*. Man had no life until his spirit was breathed into him.

God was very pleased with everything he had made (Genesis 1:31). On day seven, God rested and declared the day blessed and holy (Genesis 2:2).

The seventh day is a Sabbath to God, who made the day holy (Exodus 20:10–11). He devoted the seventh day to rest and worship. Worship above everything else maintains our connection with God and gives us a sense of belonging and a basis for our existence. We were created in innocence not knowing the difference between good and evil, but we were created knowing the difference between right and wrong.

We are the crowning glory of God's creation. We are spirits with physical bodies and souls, which comprise the mind, heart, and will; this gives us the ability to think, express feelings, and make choices. Freedom of choice lets us choose to do what is right or wrong, to obey or disobey.

God placed two trees in the middle of the garden—the Tree of Life and the Tree of the Knowledge of Good and Evil. The trees held special significance for mankind. The Tree of Life represented eternal life with God. The Tree of the Knowledge of Good and Evil represented worldly wisdom that led Adam and Eve to question or oppose God's role and authority in the established order of creation. We decide to recognize God as the ultimate authority in our lives or live according to our own rules. If we choose the latter, God becomes irrelevant in our lives.

Adam was commanded not to eat from the Tree of the Knowledge of Good and Evil upon penalty of death (Genesis 2:17). God created a wife for him (Genesis 2:21–25). Eve knew not to eat from or touch the Tree of the Knowledge of Good and Evil (Genesis 3:3).

Adam and Eve knew that disobedience to God's command would bring serious consequences. The tree presented them with the ability to exercise their free will, and they chose to disobey. They had no experience with evil before they disobeyed, and disobedience is sin. "Sin entered the world through one man, and death through sin, and in this way death came to all men, because all sinned" (Romans 5:12 NIV). Sin became a natural part of the human experience. Everyone is born predisposed to sin.

As a result of their disobedience, the Lord God said,

> The man has now become like one of us, knowing good and evil. He must not be allowed to reach out his hand and take also from the tree of life and eat, and live forever. So the Lord God banished him from the Garden of Eden to work the ground from which he had been taken (Genesis 3:22–23 NIV).

Their relationship with God was broken, and they were banished from His presence. God's judgment was swift, and spiritual death was immediate. Physical death would follow, and their actions would affect all future generations. "After he drove the man out, he placed on the east side of the Garden of Eden cherubim and a flaming sword flashing back and forth to guard the way to the tree of life" (Genesis 3:24 NIV).

Sin corrupts our spirit, soul, and body, making us impure. A barrier was needed to ensure that nothing impure could enter God's presence. This barrier included these elements.

- sword—the mouth of Christ (Revelation 1:16)
- mouth—the Word of God (Hebrews 4:12)
- word—the Word was Christ Jesus (John 1:1)

Jesus is the barrier between God and humanity. To gain access to God, we must believe in the name of Jesus and receive him as our Savior. No one comes into the presence of God without going through Jesus (John 14:6).

Summary

Only purified believers will enter heaven—nothing impure will enter (Revelation 21:26–27).

Adam and Eve were birthed by God as the central focus of His creation. They were born into a personal, loving relationship with God with the ability to think, feel, and choose. Adam and Eve made a conscious decision to disobey God.

Don't be deceived by phony words that lead to the disobedience of God's commands, resulting in his wrath (Ephesians 5:6). The sin of disobedience severed their relationship with God, and they were banished from his sight. Disobedience brought sin and evil into the world. As a result, everyone is born in sin and separated from God.

Conclusion

God does not overlook disobedience.

Questions

How is sin evidenced in the world around us?

What is the difference between right and wrong and good and evil?

CHAPTER 3

God Loves Everyone

Christians boldly declare that God loves everyone and offer John 3:16 as proof: "For God so loved the world that he gave his one and only son." The world is the totality of creation including humanity.

When Adam and Eve sinned, everything God had created became subject to destruction, decay, and death. To save humanity and creation from sin and eternal death, God was willing to sacrifice his Son on the cross for the redemption of the world: "God did not send his Son into the world to condemn the world, but to save the world through him" (John 3:17 NIV).

There was, however, one condition for humanity's salvation: "Whoever believes in him shall not perish but have eternal life" (John 3:16 NIV). We must believe in God's Son in order to be redeemed. "Whoever believes in him is not condemned" (John 3:18 NIV).

God knew before creation those who would choose to receive his Son as Lord and Savior.

- Those who receive Jesus as their Savior become the children of God (John 1:12–13).
- We are adopted into God's family through our belief in Jesus Christ (Ephesians 1:5).

- The names of those who receive Christ as their Savior were known and symbolically recorded by God; their names are recorded in heaven (Hebrews 12:23).
- Their names are recorded the Lamb's book of life (Revelation 21:27).

God also knew those who would choose to reject his Son: "But whoever does not believe stands condemned already because he has not believed in the name of God's one and only Son" (John 3:18 NIV). To be condemned means to be judged guilty and receive a heavy penalty or death sentence for something that has happened. "Whoever believes in the Son has eternal life, but whoever rejects the Son will not see life, for God's wrath remains on him" (John 3:36 NIV).

Many people labor under the false perception that they were born good and became bad. The reality is the opposite. We are born in sin; we are selfish, self-centered, and godless. We don't have to be taught these behaviors; they are inherent.

- No one is born morally virtuous (Romans 3:10).
- Everyone is born with a sin nature (Psalm 51:5).
- The sinful nature is inclined to licentious, self-centered behavior (Galatians 5:19–21).
- Our evil thoughts, attitudes, and actions originate in the heart (Mark 7:20–23).
- Our sinful nature is in opposition to God's law and cannot please Him (Romans 8:5–8).
- Because of our sin nature, we are all born spiritually dead and subject to God's wrath (Ephesians 2:1–4).

For these reasons, we must be born again: no one will see heaven unless he is born again (John 3:3); the word *unless* indicates a requirement or a condition.

There are two requirements for spiritual rebirth: "No one can enter the kingdom of heaven unless he is born of water and the Spirit"

(John 3:5 NIV). Water represents cleansing, washing away of sin, the outward symbol of deliverance. Water symbolizes the cleansing of our sin and the beginning of a new life in Christ; we are now able to enter God's presence with a good conscience (1 Peter 3:21).

Jesus provides for our redemption and the forgiveness of our sin (Colossians 1:14). We are redeemed through the blood of Jesus (Ephesians 1:7). When we are redeemed by our faith in Christ, we can receive the promised Spirit (Galatians 3:14). Like Abraham, God receives us by faith and our belief in his promises.

The Spirit is the third person of the Trinity; he intercedes for us through the sacrifice of Christ Jesus on the cross, and we have access to God by means of the Holy Spirit (Ephesians 2:18). While Jesus's sacrifice provided us access to God, the Holy Spirit provides the means of intercession and sanctification—our being made new, holy.

If we do not change our ways, we will not see heaven (Matthew 18:3). We are reborn and made new by the work of the indwelling Holy Spirit living in us (Titus 3:5).

God wants to change us from the selfish, self-centered people we are into new creations. We cannot change ourselves; the only way to achieve the kind of change God is looking for is through the work of the indwelling Holy Spirit.

- The righteous nature of the Holy Spirit stands in direct contrast to the sinful human nature (Galatians 5:17).
- The Holy Spirit empowers us to become a new person (1 Samuel 10:6).
- Through his Spirit, God will give us changed hearts (Ezekiel 36:25–27).
- The Holy Spirit strengthens us with power through our faith so Christ can live in our hearts (Ephesians 3:16–17).
- He will renew our minds and give us a new attitude (Ephesians 4:22–24).
- With transformed minds, we will be able to discern God's will (Romans 12:2).

The goal of all Christians is not to become more religious but to become more righteous, more Christlike. This involves adhering to godly principles and making choices that reflect their love for the Lord.

- The person who does what is right will become righteous (1 John 3:7).
- Righteousness leads to the holiness that result in eternal life with God (Romans 6:19–22).
- "Be Holy because I am Holy" (1 Peter 1:16 NIV).

Holiness involves seeking to reflect the character of God revealed in the person of Jesus. Holiness implies separation and purification from all that is evil or improper. The Christian community is called to avoid anything that could compromise its relationship with God.

According to Ephesians 5, we are to avoid all of these.

- sexual immorality
- impurity
- greed
- obscenity
- foolish talk
- coarse joking
- drunkenness
- debauchery
- self-indulgent behavior
- corruption
- dishonesty

"Make every effort to live in peace with all men and to be holy, without holiness no one will see the Lord" (Hebrews 12:14 NIV).

Summary

Because of Adam and Eve's disobedience, we were born with a sin nature and condemned to eternal separation from God. But God has offered humanity the way to a restored relationship with him. The requisite for restoration is belief in Christ Jesus and his sacrifice on the cross, and the condition of restoration is rebirth.

Conclusion

Because our relationship with God was severed, we must be born again; we must receive forgiveness for our sins and be filled with the Holy Spirit. If we do not have God's Holy Spirit in us, we do not belong to God (Romans 8:9). The Holy Spirit is a gift. If we have not received this gift, all we have to do is ask (Luke 11:13).

Questions

Why is rebirth necessary?

What is the goal of redemption?

CHAPTER 4

God Loves Us Equally

God does not distinguish between gender, race, nationality, appearance, intelligence, position, or power.

- Our racial, social, and gender differences are insignificant to Him (Galatians 3:28).
- God knows us through our relationship with Jesus. If we are born-again believers, we are heirs of the promise of eternal life with God through Abraham (Galatians 3:29).
- God knows the names of those who worship him and honor his name (Malachi 3:16).
- They belong to God, and they will be spared eternal punishment (Malachi 3:17).
- God does differentiate between good and evil and those who serve him and those who do not (Malachi 3:18).
- Eternal punishment awaits those who have rejected the Lord and have not served him (Malachi 4:1).

God befriends believers—those who were once his enemies but were saved from his wrath through the blood of Christ and are no longer his enemies but his friends.

- A friend is someone who stands by us (Proverbs 18:24).
- A friend is like a close relative (Ruth 2:20).
- Abraham was called God's friend (James 2:23).

Jesus told his friends there was no reason to be fearful (Luke 12:4). Unbelievers cannot claim friendship with God.

- Unbelief is sin (John 16:8–9).
- Those who do not believe in Jesus will perish because of their unbelief (John 8:24– 25).
- Unbelievers are children of the devil who reject the truth for lies (John 8:42–47).
- The minds and consciences of the unbelievers are impure and corrupt (Titus 1:15).
- Those who reject Jesus will be condemned at the final judgment (John 12:48).

Scripture refers to unbelievers as wicked and unrighteous, the opposite of morally upright and in good standing with God.

- The Lord hates the evil, arrogant and deceitful; they cannot stand in his presence (Psalm 5:4–6).
- Those who do not know God or obey the gospel will be punished (2 Thessalonians 1:8).

God gave us the Ten Commandments to serve as our moral guide. Likewise, scripture defines the behavior that God abhors (Revelation 21:8; 1 Corinthians 6:9–11). Such behavior is unacceptable to God.

We all participate in some form of godless behavior before we are saved. When we try to justify our bad behavior, we are denying our need for the Savior and reject the work of the cross. If we claim to be sinless, we deny the truth of the gospel and Jesus's sacrifice was meaningless (1 John 1:8).

Unbelieving, unrighteous, and *wicked* are words that describe the unsaved. They are strangers, friends, neighbors, and relatives. They have chosen to live by their own rules and values and outside God's authority. Scripture tells us they are godless and in need of the Savior.

They are what we once were, and we are called to reach out to them with the good news of the gospel.

God wants everyone to know the truth and be saved (1 Timothy 2:4). A day is coming when there will be a final person to be saved. We can't know who that will be or when it will occur. Therefore, as Christians, we should focus on sharing the gospel message with those around us even though we will be reviled by many. According to Luke 6:22, we are blessed when we are hated for our belief in Jesus.

Summary

There is no middle ground when it comes to our belief in Jesus. Either we believe we are sinners in need of the Savior and Jesus is our only hope of salvation, or we don't. We are either for God or against him (Matthew 12:30).

Believers are reconciled with God through Jesus's sacrifice on the cross, but there is no reconciliation for those who reject Jesus; they remain enemies of God.

We must choose between friendship with the world or with God; we can't have it both ways (James 4:4).

Conclusion

We are all born equally sinful. We are all born enemies of God. We must choose to become God's friends or remain his enemies.

Questions

Should we be able to tell if a person is a friend or an enemy of God?

How so?

CHAPTER 5

God Loves Us Unconditionally

Forgiveness from God requires the sinner's acknowledgment of him and confession of sin (1 John 1:9). God is faithful to forgive our confessed sins.

Jesus went to the cross for everyone, so everyone has the same opportunity to receive forgiveness for sin and share in God's love. "He is the atoning sacrifice for our sins, and not only for ours but also for the sins of the whole world" (1 John 2:2 NIV).

Jesus's sacrifice was sufficient for the forgiveness and restoration of everyone choosing to take advantage of the opportunity God so graciously affords all humanity.

While Jesus went to the cross for everyone, he did not die for the sins of everyone.

- He bore the sins and made intercession for many (Isaiah 53:12).
- He poured out his blood for the forgiveness of many (Matthew 26:28).
- "So Christ was sacrificed once to take away the sins of many people" (Hebrews 9:28 NIV).
- Many people who come to salvation through Jesus become part of God's family (Hebrews 2:10–11).

Many could be a large number, but it is not all. Jesus died for the sins of those who receive him as Lord and Savior; he did not die for the sins of those who reject him. Those who reject the truth of Jesus's person, sacrifice, and their need for the Savior reject God. There would be no reason for Jesus to take on the sins of those who reject him because they stand condemned already.

Casual confession lacks the sincerity and understanding needed to recognize the depth of our personal sin and the need for change in our lives.

- God is looking for spirits that are broken and hearts that are remorseful for the sins we have committed (Psalm 51:17).

- "Godly sorrow brings repentance that leads to salvation" (2 Corinthians 7:10 NIV).

Repent means to turn away from sin and to God and as well recognize the need to be changed. Recognition of our sinful state prompts repentance that leads to a restored relationship with God. Jeremiah 15:19 tells us that if we repent of our sin and change our ways, God will restore our relationship, but the word *if* is very important.

Jesus made such restoration possible by his sacrifice on the cross. We can be restored if we discontinue our previous sinful lifestyle, turn to God, and live in a way that is in accordance with his will. No one is too evil to repent (1 Kings 21:25–29).

As previously discussed, scripture is very clear about the wicked behavior the Lord will not tolerate.

- He hates pride, evil behavior, and perverted speech (Proverbs 8:13).
- He detests self-centered pride (Proverbs 16:5).
- He detests those who lie (Proverbs 12:22).
- He will respond wrathfully to self-centered people who reject his truth (Romans 2:8).

Conversely, scripture is very clear about what behavior pleases God and what repentance should look like.

- Our lives should be worthy of God—holy, righteous, and blameless (1 Thessalonians 2:10–11).
- God's grace enables us to resist worldly obsessions and live self-controlled, godly lives (Titus 2:11–12).
- Our minds should be free of worldly things and focused on love and forgiveness; we should live peaceful, grateful lives (Colossians 3:1–17).
- We should live so our lives glorify God and serve as an example for the unsaved (1 Peter 2:12–16).

God, our Father, expects faithfulness, respect, and obedience. In turn, we will enjoy his great love and compassion for eternity.

- God's great love is with those who fear—revere and respect— him (Psalm 103:11).
- God has compassion for those who fear him (Psalm 103:13).
- God loves those who fear him (Psalm 103:17).
- God loves those who keep his covenant and obey his commands (Psalm 103:18).
- God loves those who are obedient (Psalm 103:20).

Once we receive the gift of salvation, we are expected to enter and maintain a continuing relationship with Jesus through discipleship. All Christians are called to be disciples, that is, followers of Christ— his students, those who adhere to his principles.

Discipleship provides increased faith, spiritual maturity, and a deepening fellowship with the Lord. Straying from that fellowship will diminish our faith and spiritual growth and render us unsuitable for godly service.

- Spiritual maturity is a necessary component of effective godly service (Ephesians 4:11–13). The Holy Spirit will guide and teach us in all spiritual things (John 14:26).

If we are faithful to that relationship, God's Spirit will accomplish his work in us and we will produce fruit—righteous behavior that identifies us as believers.

- If we obey God's commands, we live in him and he lives in us, and we know it because his Spirit is in us (1 John 3:24).
- If we remain in God and His Spirit is in us, we will bear fruit (John 15:5).
- "But the fruit of the Spirit is love, joy, peace, patience, kindness, goodness, faithfulness, gentleness and self-control" (Galatians 5:22–23 NIV).
- "Remain in me, and I will remain in you" (John 15:4 NIV).
- "If you love me, you will obey me" (John 14:15 NIV).
- "If you obey my commands, you will remain in my love" (John 15:10 NIV).

If we remain faithful and obedient to our Lord, our relationship with him will endure. We can also reason from this verse that the opposite is true—disobedience and lack of commitment will sever our relationship with the Lord.

Summary

God sacrificed himself for our redemption, but he did not do it to the exclusion of setting conditions for his people. Our salvation is conditional; it is based on our faithfulness and obedience to God, who is faithful and will keep his covenant of love with future generations who love him and obey his commands (Deuteronomy 7:9).

There is no condemnation for those who believe and receive Jesus as Lord and Savior (Romans 8:1).

Conclusion

God has set conditions for salvation that believers are obligated to fulfill.

Question

What would happen if God had no expectations of his children?

CHAPTER 6

God Will Never Stop Loving Us

When we become part of God's family, he makes a covenant of love with us.

- Believers are God's people, and he is their God (Deuteronomy 29:12–13).
- This covenant included all future generations (Deuteronomy 29:14–15).
- The covenant is restated in the New Testament: God will be with us, and we will be his people and he will be our God (2 Corinthians 6:16).
- This covenant is conditional; it is based on our faithfulness. God will keep his covenant with those who keep his commands (Nehemiah 1:5).
- Whoever obeys his commands loves the Lord and is loved by him in return (John 14:21).
- God also made a promise to his people. Don't be afraid or discouraged; God will never leave you or forsake you (Deuteronomy 31:6–8).
- "Never will I leave you; never will I forsake you" (Hebrews 13:5 NIV).

But this is a conditional promise; the Lord will be with us if we are with him; if we earnestly seek the Lord, we will find him, and if we forsake him, he will forsake—abandon—us (2 Chronicles 15:2).

The Lord has promised never to leave us or turn his back on us, and he is looking for the same kind of commitment from us in return. Believers, however, can choose to be unfaithful and walk away from God thereby severing their relationship with the Lord. In 1 John 5:13–21 are remarks addressed to born-again believers; in 1 John 5:16, a brother—a fellow believer—can commit a sin that leads to eternal separation from God.

Sins that do not lead to death are the sins we commit against each other. If we choose to forsake God, we have committed the sin that leads to death. But if we remain faithful, Satan will not be able to harm us.

If believers take the covenant and the promise for granted and continue to live sinful lives (Deuteronomy 29:19), God will never forgive them and will blot their names out of the book of life (Deuteronomy 29:20; Exodus 32:33). This action indicates the loss of salvation.

God has known from the beginning of time the names of all who belong to him. Consequently, nowhere does scripture say that names are added to the book of life; they are only deleted.

According to Mark 3:29, if we blaspheme—that is disrespect or insult—God's Holy Spirit, we are guilty of an eternal sin. In Ezekiel 20:27, God was blasphemed when his people forsook him.

When we disrespect God's authority, ignore his Holy Spirit, and treat casually the sacrifice Jesus made for us, we commit an unforgivable sin and will lose eternal salvation.

According to Ezekiel 18:24–26, believers who are unfaithful and return to sinful lives will perish and their good works will not be remembered.

And according to Hebrews 6:4–6, it is impossible for born-again believers who have been given spiritual understanding, who have experienced heavenly peace and joy, who have been filled with the

Holy Spirit, and who recognize the truth of God's Word and his power and provision for the future to be restored to a saving relationship with God if they revert to their sinful lives because they have insulted and made a mockery of Jesus's sacrifice.

This scripture does not refer to the unsaved. Only born-again Christians can experience fellowship, peace, joy, spiritual truth, and understanding with God through the Holy Spirit. This scripture refers to the loss of salvation of born-again believers.

Hebrews 10:26–31 tells us that if we deliberately keep on sinning after we have been saved, God will reject us and we will perish with the unsaved. Saul is a prime example of the loss of salvation.

- Saul received power from the Holy Spirit (1 Samuel 10:9–10).
- Saul disobeyed God's command (1 Samuel 13:13–14).
- God was grieved (1 Samuel 15:10–11).
- God rejected Saul as king (1 Samuel 15:23).
- The Spirit of God departed from Saul (1 Samuel 16:14).
- God turned his back on Saul (1 Samuel 28:16).
- Saul perished for the sins he committed against the Lord (1 Chronicles 10:13).

King David also recognized the possibility of losing his salvation.

- He asked God not to forsake him (Psalm 27:9).
- He confessed that he had sinned against God (Psalm 51:4).
- He pleaded with God not to cast him from his presence or take away his Holy Spirit (Psalm 51:11).

"If we disown him, he will disown us" (2 Timothy 2:12 NIV); this spiritual truth is often overlooked. Sin against our fellow man is forgivable, but sin against God and the Holy Spirit is unforgiveable. The only way to restore the relationship is with a sincerely remorseful and repentant heart.

Summary

To believe that there is nothing we can do to lose our salvation suggests that God would be rendered powerless in his ability to punish persistent, deliberate disobedience. This belief sets up an imbalance of power that puts humanity in control instead of God. In 1 Peter 3:17, we are told it is better to suffer for Christ in this life than to suffer for eternity without him.

Romans 8:37–39 clearly states that no situation or person can separate us from God's love. Only we can do that by living outside of his will through rebellion and disobedience and effectively forsaking him and severing our relationship with him.

Conclusion

Salvation is a privilege, and God's love is a blessing we should not take for granted.

Question

Is it possible for a born-again Christian to sin without awareness?

CHAPTER 7

In His Name

- His name is greater than every other name (Philippians 2:9–10).
- We are baptized in his name (Acts 2:38).
- We have salvation in his name (Acts 4:12).
- We have life in his name (John 20:31).
- We gather in his name (Matthew 18:20).
- We pray in his name (John 14:13).
- God does not listen to the prayers of sinners; he hears the prayers of godly, obedient people (John 9:31).

Relationship and obedience are the conditions for answered prayer. Christ Jesus is the mediator—the link—between God and humanity who reconciles them (1 Timothy 2:5).

With cleansed hearts, belief in his Son, and lives that please God, we can have the confidence that we will receive what we ask of him (1 John 3:21–22). When we are obedient to the known will of God, he listens to and responds to our requests.

God will give us whatever we ask in Jesus's name (John 16:23).

When we pray in accordance with God's will, our prayers will be heard (1 John 5:14). We must believe that our prayers will be answered (Mark 11:24).

While God is sensitive to our personal requests, the ultimate purpose of prayer is to glorify God and accomplish his will on earth. John 14:12–14 tells us that God will answer prayers in his name.

Faith and obedience go hand in hand. When we pray in Jesus's name, we indicate our desire to be in God's will and continue the work of Christ. We believers have the same miraculous power to bring the unsaved to Christ when we identify ourselves with his name.

If we are faithful to Christ and his Word, our prayers will be answered and we will bear fruit that shows we belong to Christ (John 15:7–8). God will honor the prayers of the disciple who strives to bring others to Christ. We must abide in Christ and pray in his name to accomplish any meaningful spiritual work.

According to Ephesians 1:3, every spiritual blessing comes through our belief in the name of Jesus Christ. Ephesians 1:4 tells us that even before the creation of the world, God chose those who would believe in his Son to be made holy and blameless.

Through our belief in Jesus, we are sanctified—made holy and blameless—by the indwelling Holy Spirit. Before Creation, God chose those who would receive his Son as their Savior to become part of his family, but only believers have this privilege.

According to Ephesians 1:7, believers are redeemed and their sins are forgiven by Jesus's sacrificial blood. And Ephesians 1:9–10 says that as a result of our belief in Christ, we have been given knowledge of God's plan for the church and all humanity. His plan will be accomplished according to his purpose and will when he returns.

- Even before creation, believers were chosen and predestined to become an integral part of God's end-time plan for humanity (Ephesians 1:11).
- We who place our hope in Christ will glorify God through our belief in and faithfulness to his Son (Ephesians 1:12).
- We are saved through the truth of the gospel message of salvation (Ephesians 1:13).

- Because we believe, God seals us with the Holy Spirit (Ephesians 1:13).

Our salvation in authenticated by the indwelling of the Holy Spirit.

Summary

Jesus is the lifeline between God and us. Through Jesus alone, we can have a restored relationship and the promise of eternal life with the Lord. Every spiritual blessing is provided through Christ Jesus. With a symbolic seal, we are marked as God's possession until Christ returns.

Conclusion—Psalm 91:14–16

Because we love the Lord, acknowledge his name, and pray to him, he will

- rescue us
- protect us
- answer our prayers
- be with us in trouble
- deliver us from sin
- honor us
- provide for our salvation

Our relationship with Christ Jesus gives life value and meaning.

Question

Can you explain the reason for your faith to an unbeliever?

CHAPTER 8

When He Returns

The second coming of Christ is explained throughout the Bible. The Old Testament prophets and Jesus himself gave us detailed information about Jesus's glorious return. It will be ushered in by a cosmic disturbance the likes of which have never been seen before.

- The day the Lord returns will be different from any other day, known only to the Lord. The day will usher in perpetual light without time or weather. Christ will be the source of light and life, and he will rule over the earth as the one true God (Zechariah 14:6–9).
- When the tribulation ends, there will be a great cosmic disturbance—the sun and moon will cease to give light, and the stars will disappear from the sky (Matthew 24:29).
- Christ will appear in the sky coming on the clouds (Matthew 24:30).
- The seventh trumpet will sound, and voices will announce Christ's return (Revelation 11:15).
- Every eye will witness the return of Christ, even those who crucified him (Revelation 1:7).
- "And the glory of the Lord will be revealed, and all mankind together will see it. For the mouth of the Lord has spoken" (Isaiah 40:5 NIV).

The heavens and earth will pass away (Matthew 24:35), and this is how that will happen.

- There will be a great earthquake and a severe hailstorm (Revelation 11:19).
- People will flee to caverns and caves out of fear of the Lord as the earth is shaken at his return (Isaiah 2:19–21).
- People will beg for the mountains and hills to fall on them (Luke 23:30).
- People hiding in the caves will cry out for the mountains to fall on them (Revelation 6:15–17).
- Valleys and mountains will be made level (Isaiah 40:4).
- Believers need not fear when the earth gives way (Psalm 46:2).
- The earth will be broken apart, split, and shaken (Isaiah 24:19).

The only way for everyone to see and hear the Lord at the same time is for the earth to be made flat. People won't see the Lord's return on electronic devices; they will be watching this phenomenon in person.

- The Lord's voice will shake the earth and heavens, and he will remove what he has created (Hebrews 12:26).
- The Lord's voice will roar from on high, and he will bring judgment on all humanity (Jeremiah 25:30–31).
- His voice will strike like lightning and twist the trees and strip them bare (Psalm 29:7–9).
- Everyone in graves will hear him and come out to face judgment (John 5:28–29).

The living and the dead will hear the powerful and authoritative voice of the Lord. "At the name of Jesus every knee should bow, in heaven and on earth and under the earth, and every tongue confess that Jesus Christ is Lord, to the glory of God the Father" (Philippians 2:10–11 NIV).

When Christ returns, judgment will come and the Lord will reign with his church on Mount Zion (Isaiah 24:21–23).

When the Lord comes in power, he will bring his reward with him—eternal life in heaven with him for those who were faithful to him (Isaiah 40:10). He will gather his church to spend eternity with him (Matthew 24:31).

According to Matthew 24:6–31, certain things will happen before his return.

- Wars and rumors of wars will be prevalent.
- Earthquakes and famines will occur.
- Christians will be persecuted and hated because of Jesus.
- Many will turn away from the faith.
- Wickedness will increase.
- False prophets will deceive many.
- The antichrist will be revealed.
- Persecution will be unequaled in extent.
- Persecution will be cut short, and Christ will return for the church

Christians are told not to be afraid; these things must happen (Matthew 24:6).

Summary

When the Lord returns, "The heavens will disappear with a roar; the elements will be destroyed by fire, and the earth and everything in it will be laid bare" (2 Peter 3:10 NIV).

Eventually, the world as we know it will be brought to ruin (Hebrews 12:27–28). God will destroy all he has created. But born-again Christians are part of God's unshakable kingdom built on a solid foundation that cannot be destroyed.

Conclusion

Everyone will witness Christ's return with reverence and respect. No one will fail to notice the significance of this event.

Question

With the world in turmoil, where should Christians focus their attention before Christ returns?

CHAPTER 9

We Will Be Judged

There are three battles mentioned in the book of Revelation. The first battle details Satan's expulsion from heaven.

Just prior to his crucifixion, Jesus announced that Satan's reign on earth was about to begin (John 14:30).

Jesus's crucifixion began at the third hour. Darkness came over the land from the sixth to the ninth hour, and Jesus died at the ninth hour (Mark 15:25–37).

The fourth trumpet coincides with Jesus's crucifixion—a third of the day and night were without light (Revelation 8:12).

Revelation 12:5 describes Jesus's birth and resurrection, and to add more information, Revelation 12:7–9 tells us there was war in heaven. Satan and his angels were defeated by Michael and his angels and hurled to earth.

The timing of Satan's expulsion from heaven is significant because Satan, who represents death, could not coexist in heaven with the risen Christ, who defeated death.

The second battle, the Battle of Armageddon, will follow Christ's return and the rapture of the church.

- The dead in Christ will be raised (the first resurrection) to live with Christ (Revelation 20:4).

- In concert with the raising of the dead in Christ, living believers (the church) will be raptured to live with Christ (1 Corinthians 15:50–54).
- Satan, the antichrist, and the false prophet will gather their unsaved followers for the Battle of Armageddon (Revelation 16:13–16).
- Christ will appear with the church ready to do battle with the unsaved nations (Revelation 19:11–15).
- The antichrist and his army will prepare to battle Christ and his army (Revelation 19:19).

However, there will be no battle. The antichrist and the false prophet will be thrown into hell, and the army of the unsaved will be killed (Revelation 19:20).

Satan will be bound and thrown into the abyss to be released after 1,000 years (Revelation 20:1–3). During those 1,000 years, the Millennium, the church will live with Christ in peace and safety.

The third battle will occur at the end of the Millennium after Satan is released from the abyss. At the end of the 1,000 years, the unsaved will be raised from the dead (the second resurrection) and Satan will be released from the abyss and gather the nations from Gog (a place and another name for Satan) to Magog for the final confrontation with Christ (Revelation 20:5–8).

Christ will bring a sword against Gog (Ezekiel 38:14–22). He will execute judgment on him and pour torrents of rain, hailstone, and burning sulfur on him and his troops.

But once again, there will be no battle. Satan will be thrown into the lake of burning sulfur and suffer eternal torment in hell (Revelation 20:10).

Following Satan's defeat, God will preside over the final judgment.

- God will take his seat on his throne and the books will be opened (Daniel 7:9–10).
- Christ will appear and be given full power and authority to judge (Daniel 7:13–14).
- When Christ appears, he will sit on his throne with the nations gathered before him. The saved—the sheep—will be on the right, and the unsaved—the goats—will be on the left (Matthew 25:31–33).
- Two books will be opened—the book of death and the book of life (Revelation 20:12). The dead—the unsaved—will be judged first, and the sea, death, and Hades—where unsaved souls will reside until the final judgment—will give up the dead (Revelation 20:13).
- Each person will be judged, not for the sins they committed but for rejecting Christ; the unsaved will enter hell at the same time (Matthew 25:41).
- The unsaved will be cast into the lake of fire, known as the second death (Revelation 20:14), where there is conscious suffering for eternity (Mark 9:48).
- Anyone whose name is not found in the book of life will be cast into hell (Revelation 20:15).
- He will tell those on his right to claim their eternal inheritance in heaven promised to them before creation (Matthew 25:34).

The church will enter heaven as the unified body of Christ. Judgment for the saved and unsaved will be swift and irreversible.

Christ Jesus will have the final say. There will be no review of our accomplishments. If we are known by Jesus, we will spend eternity with him. If he does not know us, we will perish.

According to Matthew 7:21–23, not everyone who claims the name of the Lord will enter heaven. Church attendance and good works are meaningless outside a personal relationship with Jesus and the guidance of the Holy Spirit.

The blessing of creature comforts does not mean we have found favor with God. An occasional thoughtful word or deed does not mean we have a relationship with the Lord. Christian activity is not necessarily inspired by the Holy Spirit. Those who preach and teach can have hearts that are hardened toward the truth.

Summary

Our purpose on earth is to glorify God, not ourselves. What others think of us is irrelevant. The only opinion that matters is God's.

Ecclesiastes 3:17 tells us God will judge all people—the righteous and the evil (2 Corinthians 5:10).

Judgment will take place on earth. When we draw our last breaths, our final destination will be determined.

If you hear God's voice, don't ignore his call (Hebrews 4:7).

Conclusion

God calls us all to himself. We all receive the opportunity to accept or reject God's offer of salvation; the choice is ours.

If we are faithful, the Lord will be with us and will save us. He will take care of us and quiet us with his love. He will express his joy with singing (Zephaniah 3:17).

Questions

Can it get any better than that?

Have you made your choice?

Printed in the United States
By Bookmasters